THE MAGIC SHOW REVIEW

Written by
Sharon New

Illustrated by
Kelvin Hucker

Contents

Chapter 1 Meg Billboard's Reviews 3

Chapter 2 The Marvellous Moustachio? 6

Chapter 3 Disastrous Magic Tricks 11

Chapter 4 The Review 19

Chapter 1

Meg Billboard's Reviews

Meg Billboard's job was to write reviews of shows for the newspaper. People read her reviews to find out if they would enjoy going to see a show.

Meg wrote about what she enjoyed in a show. She also wrote about what she didn't like in a show. People enjoyed reading her reviews in the newspaper.

At work, Meg read one of her reviews in the newspaper. It was about a ballet dance she had seen last night. She had not enjoyed the ballet!

MEG BILLBOARD

Reviews The Ballet Dance

What did I think of the ballet dance? It was so boring I fell asleep during the dance! The ballet dancers were bad. The music was horrible. I did not enjoy the show.

Meg went to the newspaper editor's office.

"What shows can I write about tonight?" she asked the editor.

"There's a circus at the park tonight," said the editor. Meg screwed up her face.

"There's an opera at the opera house," said the editor. Meg rolled her eyes. "There's a magic show at the theatre." Meg didn't enjoy magic shows either. But it would be easy to write a funny review, she thought.

"I'll review the magic show," said Meg.

Chapter **2**

The Marvellous Moustachio?

That night, Meg went to the magic show. From her seat in the front row, she saw a magician's table on stage.

"Ladies and gentlemen," said a voice. "Would you please welcome the magnificent, the magical, the marvellous ... Moustachio!"

The audience clapped loudly. But Meg Billboard didn't clap. She knew she wouldn't use 'marvellous', 'magnificent' or 'magical' in her review of the show.

The curtains on the stage rustled and ruffled.
But Moustachio did not appear.

"He can't even make himself appear!"
said someone in the audience, laughing.
Meg Billboard smiled to herself.

Finally, Moustachio the Magician appeared from *under* the curtain! He hadn't been able to find his way out! He stood up and bowed. His face was red and he looked nervous.

"For my first trick, I will make a white rabbit appear from my top hat."

He took off his top hat and put it on the table. He tapped it with his magic wand. The audience watched quietly. Meg Billboard waited to see what would happen.

Nothing happened! Someone in the audience started to laugh. Moustachio tapped the hat three more times. Still, nothing happened. Meg Billboard knew what she was going to write about *this* magic show!

"It's a disappearing rabbit," said someone else from the audience.

Moustachio looked into the hat.

"I seem to have lost my rabbit," he said in a surprised voice.

Everyone in the audience laughed. Meg Billboard laughed, too. She began to enjoy herself. She was going to write a very bad review!

Chapter 3
Disastrous Magic Tricks

"For my next trick, I need a credit card. Does anyone have one?" asked Moustachio.

Meg Billboard stood up and gave Moustachio her credit card.

"Don't make *that* disappear!" said Meg. The audience laughed.

Moustachio cut Meg's credit card in half. Meg and the rest of the audience looked nervous. Moustachio the Magician tried *not* to look nervous!

"I will put both pieces into my magic box. They will magically reappear as a whole credit card!" said Moustachio.

Moustachio dropped the pieces of plastic into a box on the table, closed the lid, and tapped it with his wand.

He held the box upside down, and opened it. The audience watched quietly.

Instead of a whole credit card, the two cut-up halves clattered onto the floor.

Everyone laughed and laughed, except Meg. Moustachio stared at the floor.

Meg Billboard glared at Moustachio. The audience clapped and cheered and laughed louder than before.

Moustachio looked nervously at the audience. None of his magic tricks were working.

"The scarf trick!" he said loudly. "From my hand, many colourful scarves will appear!"

He started to pull the scarves out of his sleeve. Then, with a loud tearing sound, his whole sleeve came off.

The audience clapped and cheered and laughed again.

Even Meg Billboard laughed loudly, and forgot about her credit card.

"The coin trick!" said Moustachio. He was sure that *this* trick would work! He asked a man to join him on stage.

The trick was to make a coin appear from behind the man's ear. But just as he pulled the coin out from behind the man's ear, something terrible happened.

The button on Moustachio's shirt sleeve became caught in the man's hair. As he threw the coin up into the air, he saw that the man's hair was a wig! And it was caught on his button!

Moustachio and the bald man both looked shocked.

The audience laughed and laughed again. Meg Billboard was laughing so much, tears rolled down her cheeks.

"I can saw people in half," said Moustachio nervously. "Will someone from the audience join me on stage?"

"You must be joking!" they called out, in between their laughter.

Moustachio looked around the audience sadly. He walked off the stage, looking very upset.

Chapter 4
The Review

Meg Billboard stood up, still laughing, and went home. She began to write her review. But, no matter how hard she tried, she couldn't write a bad review. She decided to change all the words that described how bad Moustachio's show was. Instead, she wrote words that described how good the show was.

She had actually enjoyed Moustachio's muddled show. She had not laughed so much in a long time.

Meg finished writing her review with a big smile on her face.

MEG BILLBOARD

Reviews The Moustachio Magic Show

What did I think of the show? This is the best show in town! Moustachio's magic tricks will make you laugh and laugh. Buy your tickets now. Don't miss the show. Moustachio is a magnificent, magical, marvellous comedian!

The next day, people read Meg Billboard's review in the newspaper. Everyone wanted to see the best show in town.

Two days later, Meg picked up the newspaper and saw a photo of Moustachio.

Underneath the photo, she read about how Moustachio would perform his show for another two weeks! He was famous!

"Well, well," said Meg, as she read on, smiling.

"Extended by Popular Demand! As Recommended by Meg Billboard! Moustachio, the Magical Comedian! The Best Show in Town!"

Just then, the phone rang.

"Meg Billboard? This is Mrs Moustachio speaking. I just wanted to say a really big thank you for writing an excellent review of my husband's show. He was very upset that his magic tricks didn't work—but now *everybody* wants to see his show!"

"I'm pleased for you both," said Meg.

"As a thank-you gift, we'd like to give you some free tickets. Would you like to come to tonight's show?"

Meg Billboard knew what other shows were on that night. There was a play. There was another ballet. There was a new movie. But Meg had made up her mind.

"Mrs Moustachio," she said, smiling. "I'd love to come!"

Meg put down the phone and felt pleased that she had helped Moustachio.

"Let's hope that none of his magic tricks work tonight," she said to herself, chuckling. "That *would* spoil the show!"